The Song of the Nightingale

Inspired by the life of Saint Francis of Assisi

Written and illustrated by
Fiona French

Blackie

Saint Francis was nearing the end of a long journey.
He was glad to be coming home to Assisi, but as he
approached the town he saw an army from Perugia
camped outside the walls, and his heart grew heavy.
Why were the two towns always at war?

Saint Francis went into Assisi and tried to talk to the people.

'Why must you always be fighting?' he asked. 'War brings nothing but misery. Why don't you put away your swords and live in peace with the people of Perugia?'

But all the people turned their backs, went into their houses and closed the shutters.

Saint Francis climbed the steep road to the castle and
begged the Lords of Assisi to end the war.

'Where you lead, your people will follow,' he said.
'Why do you always lead them into war?'
But the Lords of Assisi simply turned away.

Sadly Saint Francis made his way out of the town. At
the gates he met his mother who had brought him
some bread and wine.

'You will never make the people listen,' she said.
'They have been at war with Perugia all their lives.

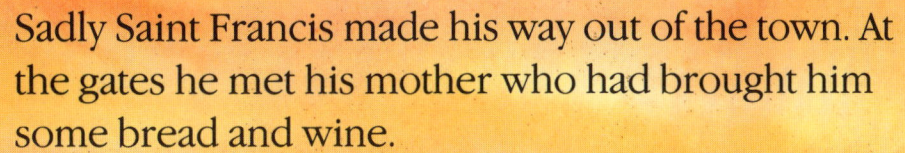

Saint Francis sat on the hill overlooking Assisi and watched the armies preparing for battle. He felt so helpless – there was nothing he could do to stop them.

And then, suddenly, he heard the first clear notes of a nightingale's evening song. Saint Francis looked up into the trees and called to the little bird.

'Brother Nightingale, your song is so beautiful – come with me into Assisi and let the people hear you sing.'
The little bird flew down onto his hand, and Saint Francis carried him back into the town.

The nightingale's beautiful song reached
every corner of the town, and pierced
every stone wall and every closed
door. And the people in the town
came to their windows, opened
their shutters and listened.
The song touched their
hearts and made them
see how they hated war.

Then Saint Francis took the nightingale to the Perugian army gathered on the plain. The little bird sang once again and the fierce soldiers stood still and listened. They could no longer think of battle.

Even the Perugian general stopped his horse
and listened.

The sweet sound of the nightingale's song pierced his heart and made him think of his home and his family waiting for his return. Suddenly he realized that he did not want to lead his army into battle.

The next morning, instead of the cries of battle, shouts of joy filled the streets of Assisi. The general of Perugia and the ruling Lord of Assisi met and promised never again to fight each other.

Assisi was at peace. The nightingale flew back into the
forest and Saint Francis set out once more on his
journeys to distant lands.